Ultimate Cars

BEETLE

Jill C. Wheeler

ABDO

VISIT US AT
WWW.ABDOPUB.COM

Published by ABDO Publishing Company, 4940 Viking Drive, Suite 622, Edina, Minnesota 55435. Copyright ©2004 by Abdo Consulting Group, Inc. International copyrights reserved in all countries. No part of this book may be reproduced in any form without written permission from the publisher.

Printed in the United States.

Edited by: Melanie A. Howard
Interior Production and Design: Terry Dunham Incorporated
Cover Design: Mighty Media
Photos: Corbis, Ron Kimball Photography

Library of Congress Cataloging-in-Publication Data

Wheeler, Jill C., 1964-
    Beetle / Jill C. Wheeler.
        p. cm. -- (Ultimate Cars)
    Includes index.
    ISBN 1-59197-578-6
    1. Volkswagen Beetle automobile--History--Juvenile literature. 2. Volkswagen automobiles--History--Juvenile literature. [1. Volkswagen Beetle automobile--History.] I. Title. II. Series.

TL215.V6W49 2004
629.222'2--dc22

2003065513

Contents

The People's Car

The Bug. The Beetle. The Vee-Dub. The New Beetle. Call it what you like. It is the best-selling car ever produced. The first Beetle roared into life in Germany in the 1930s. Over the years, the Beetle has evolved from a joke to a beloved classic. More than 20 million Beetles have been sold around the globe. The Beetle is among the most recognized products in history. Its familiar shape has been second only to the Coca-Cola bottle in consumer recognition.

Engineers began developing the beloved, curvy Beetle in the early 1930s. From the beginning, the Beetle was meant to be a very different kind of car. It was supposed to be a car for regular people, not just rich people. In fact, *Volkswagen* even means "people's car" in the German language.

The dream for a people's car came from an unlikely source. German dictator Adolph Hitler loved cars even though he never learned to drive. His first public speech as chancellor of Germany was at the Berlin Auto Show in February 1933. Hitler told the German people he would build a system of roads called the *autobahn*. He told them he would make it easier for everyone to drive. And he talked of a car people could buy for fewer than 1,000 marks.

In his dream to make a people's car, Hitler found a partner. It was Austrian-born auto designer Dr. Ferdinand Porsche. In the 1930s, Porsche was already working on a design for a *Kleinauto*, or little car. He met with Hitler to sketch out a plan for a people's car. Hitler promised that the German government would give Porsche money for the project.

Design plans turned into prototype cars in 1936. Prototypes are early versions of a car. These cars featured the rounded lines of what would become the Beetle. The prototypes changed again in 1937. Now they had shortened rear-side windows.

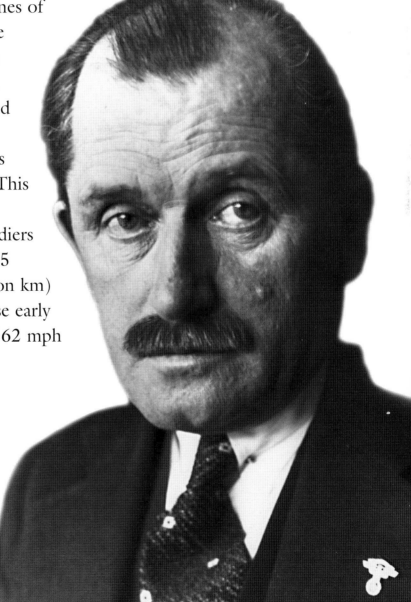

These last prototypes had to be test-driven. This job fell to Hitler's own soldiers. Some 200 soldiers drove the prototypes 1.5 million miles (2.4 million km) around Germany. These early cars had a top speed of 62 mph (99 km/h).

Ferdinand Porsche in 1934

KdF Wagens

Porsche was confident of his design by 1937. Now it was time to think about building cars. The German government gave Porsche the money to build a town and a factory near Fallersleben, Germany. It was called KdF-Stadt. Hitler laid the first stone for the new plant in May 1938. The factory would produce the KdF car.

KdF stood for the *Kraft durch Freude* movement. It means "strength through joy" in German. The movement was started to organize recreational activities for workers. Money from the KdF fund was used to build Porsche's factory. KdF was also Hitler's name for his people's car project. But the name never caught on with the factory workers. They called the car the Volkswagen. The name stuck.

Workers began building KdF wagens in 1938. By this time, Porsche had added a rear window to his design. He also recessed the headlights so that they were even with the fenders. The finished KdF wagen made its first appearance at the 1939 Berlin Auto Show. It would look much the same for the next 50 years.

Car production stalled in the fall of 1939. Hitler's armies invaded Eastern Europe, and World War II began. Hitler made the KdF-Stadt factory change so that it could build military vehicles. Workers had built just 210 cars before the war began. None of them went to ordinary German citizens.

Because the factory at KdF-Stadt was producing military vehicles, it became a key target for Allied bombers. Three bombing runs in April 1944, left the plant badly damaged. When the war ended in May 1945, only about one-third of the factory was still standing. U.S. troops occupied KdF-Stadt for a short while after the war and renamed the town Wolfsburg.

In July 1945, the Americans called Porsche to Frankfurt, Germany. He was questioned about ties to the Nazi Party, even though he stayed out of politics. However, Porsche spent almost two years in a French prison. Porsche never had anything to do with KdF cars again.

The first chapter in the Beetle's story was over. The second chapter would be written by a different group of people. Their efforts would make automotive history.

Building Cars At Last

The Allied victory in World War II in 1945 left Germany divided into four zones. U.S. soldiers were stationed in one of the zones. The Soviet Union and France controlled two other zones. Great Britain controlled the fourth. The Wolfsburg plant was in the British zone. British soldiers found themselves in charge of a badly damaged factory and hundreds of starving auto workers.

British forces quickly turned the plant into a repair facility for their vehicles. Meanwhile, factory workers salvaged the production equipment. The workers used the equipment to start building KdF cars again. They built an amazing 1,785 cars by the end of the year. They traded the cars to British troops for food and other supplies. The German workers continued their cars-for-food plan through 1947.

In 1948, the British tried to sell the plant to Henry Ford II, but Ford said no. Then British officials thought about tearing down the plant. But they changed their minds and turned the factory over to Heinz Nordhoff instead. Nordhoff had been a German automotive executive with Adam Opel AG, the European General Motors operation. Now he needed a job. The Wolfsburg plant gave him one.

Nordhoff made the plant more productive. He slashed the time and money needed to build each car. He rewarded workers who helped make the building process better. Nordhoff worked to improve quality and durability. Many people pressured him to change the car's design. They were afraid people would see the chubby car and think of Hitler. Nordhoff refused and stuck to Porsche's original KdF design, even though other car companies changed their designs every year. It was a new way of thinking that paid off.

By July 1953, the Wolfsburg plant had built 500,000 cars. By then, the Federal Republic of Germany owned the factory. Hitler's KdF name was long gone, and the Volkswagen name was firmly in place. Some 70,000 Volkswagens had been sold outside Germany, mainly in Belgium, Sweden, and Switzerland. Only about 2,000 of the six million cars sold in the United States that year were Volkswagens, though. The company had yet to establish itself across the Atlantic. However, it would soon.

America

The efforts of early Volkswagen dealers in the United States were unsuccessful. The models that had made it to the United States sold quickly, but American dealers just were not excited about the cars. The only real fans were World War II veterans who had driven the cars in Europe.

The few American car buyers who wanted a Volkswagen in the early 1950s had four choices. The standard Beetle sedan, as the KdF car was now named, sold for $1,295. The DeLuxe sold for $1,480. It had hydraulic brakes and upgraded interiors and exteriors. A Beetle with a sunroof cost $1,550. Though convertibles were rare in the United States, it was possible to get one for just under $2,400.

Volkswagen executives wanted to boost their sales in the United States. They knew that they needed a different way of doing business to achieve this goal. The problem that Americans had with Volkswagens was that parts had to be imported from Europe. This took time and was expensive. Also, very few American mechanics knew how to fix them. So Nordhoff decided to put a Volkswagen branch in the United States to solve both issues. The plan worked. Volkswagen was America's top-selling import by the end of 1954.

It helped that Volkswagen had more to offer by then. The engine had been enlarged from 1.1 liter to almost 1.2 liter. The change boosted the engine's horsepower from 30 hp to 36 hp. A single oval rear window had replaced the split window. Drivers could start the car with a key-type starter switch. Before, they had used a dashboard push button. Also, the engine no longer required a break-in period.

Some parts of the Beetle were still less than perfect, though. Beetle owners enjoyed bragging that their air-cooled engines did not need antifreeze. However, that also meant there was no coolant to flow through the heater hoses. Beetle heaters functioned poorly, if at all. The design left winter drivers bundled up and shivering!

A new American plant.

After 27 years (and nearly 6 million VWs) in the U.S.A., we feel enough at home here to make a home here.

So we've opened a factory in Westmoreland, Pennsylvania, to make VW Rabbits as fast and as well as we know how.

Over the past years, you've found that we make good products. Over the coming years, you'll find that we make good corporate citizens, too.

Long ago, someone said, "I don't want an imported car. I want a Volkswagen."

How wunderbar that it turned out to be true.

This advertisement announces that Volkswagen will be making cars in the United States.

The Convertible Craze

Convertibles were nothing new to Volkswagen. A convertible had been present at the cornerstone ceremony at the Wolfsburg plant in 1938. Convertibles also had been built for British officers after the war. Volkswagen began building Beetle convertibles at the Karmann coachwork firm in 1949. These early models were a welcome change for convertible fans. They featured bulky soft tops, oversized rear windows, and extra padding for sound absorption.

Before 1955, few Beetle convertibles had appeared on the American market. That soon changed. Convertibles became more and more popular over the next 10 years. Convertible Beetles usually had more features than standard Beetles. They also had a higher price tag. Engineers had increased the convertible engine size by 1966. The new 50 hp, 1.3-liter engine helped the car haul the added weight of the heavy ragtop.

Only movie stars and true convertible fans bought Beetle convertibles at first. However, that market had expanded by the late 1960s. Convertible advertising bragged about drivers getting tan as they drove. Other ads hinted that it was easier for men to get dates when they drove a convertible.

The Beetle convertible became very popular in the United States in the 1960s.

The Car of the 60s

The Beetle changed little on the outside between its U.S. introduction in the 1950s and the early 1960s. A larger, square window in the back of the 1958 models was the biggest difference. The window replaced the smaller oval window that limited visibility and bothered some drivers. This new feature, along with a larger windshield, gave drivers a broader range of vision. Drivers also enjoyed a flat gas pedal. They had used a roller-type accelerator in the older models.

Beetle demand was steady and strong. But Dr. Carl Hahn thought it could be better. Hahn had become head of Volkswagen America in 1959. He put Volkswagen on the road toward its first major advertising campaign that year. The campaign was different from other car campaigns. It made fun of the Beetle's size. It also made fun of the fact that the overall design never changed. At the same time, it highlighted the car's many quality checks. The campaign also talked about the car's cutting edge engineering.

The ad campaign helped give the curvy little Beetle more personality. Many owners already thought of their Beetles as a part of the family. If anything, the attitudes of the 1960s and early 1970s strengthened that feeling. The Beetle was the perfect vehicle for this "new" generation of Americans.

Lemon.

This Volkswagen missed the boat.

The chrome strip on the glove compartment is blemished and must be replaced. Chances are you wouldn't have noticed it; Inspector Kurt Kroner did.

There are 3,389 men at our Wolfsburg factory with only one job: to inspect Volkswagens at each stage of production. (3000 Volkswagens are produced daily; there are more inspectors than cars.)

Every shock absorber is tested (spot checking won't do), every windshield is scanned. VWs have been rejected for surface scratches barely visible to the eye.

Final inspection is really something! VW inspectors run each car off the line onto the Funktionsprüfstand (car test stand), tote up 189 check points, gun ahead to the automatic brake stand, and say "no" to one VW out of fifty.

This preoccupation with detail means the VW lasts longer and requires less maintenance, by and large, than other cars. (It also means a used VW depreciates less than any other car.)

We pluck the lemons; you get the plums.

Volkswagen used humor in its advertisements. In reality, the Beetle was no lemon. These cars went through many inspections at the factory.

They thought for themselves. They appreciated good, simple things. Buying a Beetle had always been a little unusual. Owning a Beetle helped make nonconformists even more different from the rest of society.

Beetles quickly became more than cars to this generation. They became a symbol of the times. Beetle owners painted their cars in bright, brilliant colors. They had contests to see how many people they could fit in a Beetle. Some changed their Beetles into horse-drawn carriages and dune buggies. Beetle fans even held contests to see how far a Beetle would float in the water. Beetles appeared in art, music, and movies like Walt Disney's *The Love Bug*.

And all the while the car was being improved. By 1964, the Beetle's four-cylinder rear engine had increased to 40 hp.

Owners who wanted to stand out sometimes painted amusing designs on their Beetles.

It would increase again in 1970 to 57 hp. The car now had a front anti-sway bar to improve cornering. It had been added in 1960. The next year the gas tank was flattened to increase luggage volume, too. In 1968, Volkswagen finally decided to make Beetles with an automatic transmission to compete with the other car companies. The company started producing Beetles with what they called an Automatic Stick Shift. The transmission was not completely automatic. However, gears could be shifted without using a clutch.

Pit Stop

Beetle stuffing was a popular activity in the 1960s and 1970s. A new generation took up Beetle stuffing after the release of the New Beetle in 1998.

Super Beetles

The U.S. auto market changed in the early 1970s. The nation was caught in a fuel shortage. Spiking gas prices made smaller, more fuel-efficient cars more popular. Other companies began focusing on the growing small-car market. Ford introduced the Pinto. Chevrolet came out with the Vega. The Beetle also had to compete with more Japanese imports than before. These cars came from companies like Honda and Toyota. This battle for consumers cut into Beetle sales.

To compete in this crowded market, Volkswagen introduced the Super Beetle in 1971. The Super Beetle lived up to its name. It had a bigger trunk and a new, coil-spring front suspension with MacPherson struts. This change reduced the car's turning circle by more than four feet (one m). The $2,299 Super Beetle featured a larger, 1.6-liter engine and had a top speed of 83 mph (132 km/h).

The Super Beetle gave Volkswagen a boost in sales. With both the Super Beetle and the standard Beetle being sold on the American market, Volkswagen reached a new production record in 1972. The company had now built more than 15,007,034 Beetles. This beat the old production record held by the Ford Model T. The Beetle was now the most-produced car in the world.

In spite of this success, Beetle demand began to slow in the early 1970s. Volkswagen tried to fight back with some special editions of the Beetle. The Sports Bug appeared in 1973. It had beltline striping and black bumpers and trim. It offered an Indy-type steering wheel and contoured bucket seats. This gave drivers more of a racecar feel.

The following year, the Sun Bug appeared. It had gold metallic paint and a beefed-up interior. Sun Bug advertising promised more smiles and sunny days for drivers.

The Love Bug, named after Herbie from the 1969 Disney movie, was introduced in mid-1974. It featured a special price of $2,524, and was available in red or green. Volkswagen then introduced the La Grande Bug in 1975. It was flashier, with metallic paint, sport wheels, and a leather-grained interior.

Herbie the Love Bug

End of an Era

Even with the introduction of new models, Beetle sales continued to slip throughout the 1970s. Volkswagen stopped building Beetles at the Wolfsburg plant in July 1974. The plant began building the Volkswagen Golf and the Rabbit instead. The last year for Super Beetle sales was 1975. All Beetles produced after that had the original Porsche design.

Standard Beetle sales in the United States ended in 1977. Fewer than 20,000 Beetles were sold that year. Some 90,000 Beetles had been sold in the United States just three years earlier. The Beetle convertible hung on for two more years.

Beetle production left Germany altogether in 1978 and moved to Mexico. The Mexican plant continued to make the original Beetle for many years. The car was no longer sold in the United States. However, other nations kept buying the Beetle. Even today, many taxis in Mexico are Beetles.

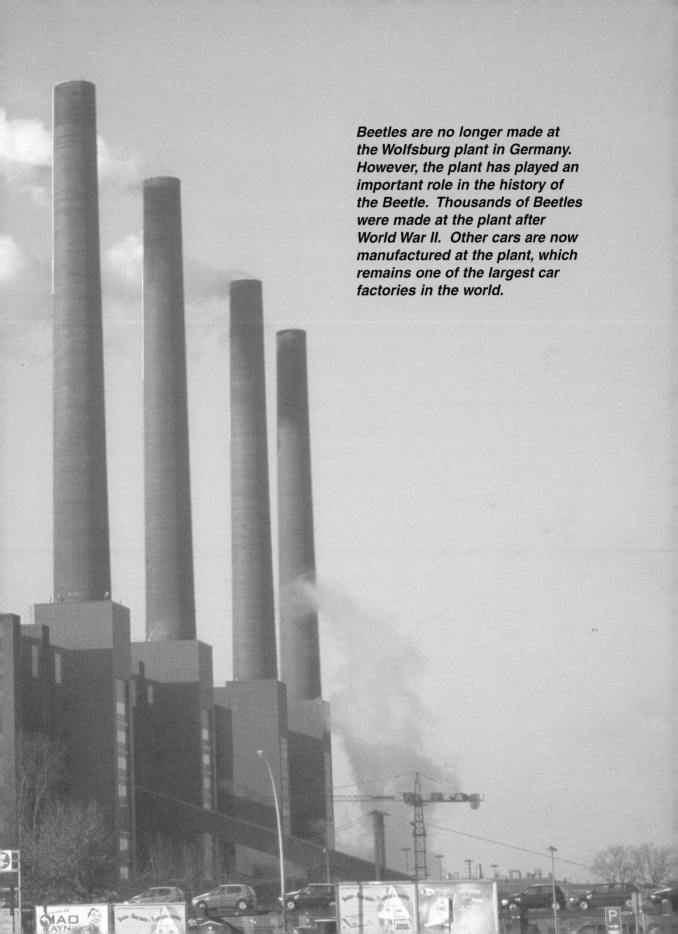

Beetles are no longer made at the Wolfsburg plant in Germany. However, the plant has played an important role in the history of the Beetle. Thousands of Beetles were made at the plant after World War II. Other cars are now manufactured at the plant, which remains one of the largest car factories in the world.

Beetle Racing

Even though Americans could not buy new Beetles after 1977, Beetle fans maintained interest in the car. They created a thriving second-hand market. Beetle buffs continued to collect and trade vehicles.

Some companies took advantage of the trend. They were set up to convert Beetles into racing cars. They added anti-roll bars, stabilizer bars, and camber compensators. These things were great for drivers looking to soup up their Beetle.

In fact, people turned standard Beetles into many different cars. Dune Buggies, "Cal-look" Beetles, and hot rods are just a few. Even early Formula Vee racers were basically the same loveable bug underneath, with almost the same 1.2-liter engine, transmission, and brakes.

Like Herbie the Love Bug, Beetles did well in endurance racing. People laughed at first when Beetles entered races. They were racing against more expensive cars with more horsepower. Race fans stopped laughing as the Bugs piled up wins. In the 1960s, Beetles won both the Baja 500 and the Mexican 1000 off-road races. Volkswagen issued a Baja Champion SE model in 1971 in honor of the tough cars.

Beetles proved that they could be fast and sturdy by winning races. Drivers won endurance races in Mexico with Beetles. Racing spectators also could see Beetles speeding down drag strips.

A New Beginning

By 1994, the Beetle had been missing from American car lots for 17 years. Volkswagen had continued to sell other models in the United States. But none approached the cult status of the Beetle. Volkswagen had remained the number one European car manufacturer but was considered only a minor player in the United States.

Volkswagen had a surprise in store at the 1994 North American International Auto Show. Show attendees saw a vaguely familiar sight at the Volkswagen exhibit. It was a concept car that looked a little like the old Beetle. It had the same simple, friendly shape. The car almost begged people to hug it.

The concept car drew a lot of attention. Volkswagen took notice. The New Beetle moved from concept to reality in four short years.

The New Beetle began as a secret project called Concept 1. It was based in Volkswagen's California Design Studio. The studio was under the direction of Freeman Thomas and J. Mays. Thomas had been a designer for Porsche. Mays would go on to become chief designer at Ford. The two listened to Volkswagen's objective for Concept 1. Quite simply, the company wanted to get back into the American market. Thomas and Mays suggested Volkswagen bring back the Beetle.

Mays, Thomas, and their design team began working to create a new version of the old favorite. They tried to think of words to describe the feeling they wanted to evoke in people who saw the car. Words like honest, simple, and emotional surfaced repeatedly. The team also looked at shapes for the car. Team members tossed different shapes onto a table. They moved them around and discarded those they did not like. The circle won.

Designing the New Beetle took only three days. Selling the idea to Volkswagen's German executives took years. This new Beetle would be very different from the old one. In fact, in many ways it would be the opposite. The New Beetle was front-wheel drive and front-engined. It was liquid-cooled, not air-cooled. It was a hatchback, not a two-door. It would also be more high tech. New Beetle drivers would enjoy airbags, a CD player, and power steering. They would also have a heater that worked.

The Beetle is Back

The New Beetle hit American car lots in 1998. It was made in Volkswagen's Puebla, Mexico, plant. Designers of the New Beetle wanted the car to be slightly smaller. However, they had to build it on the Golf platform. The New Beetle was therefore larger than the original.

The New Beetle featured a 2.0-liter/115 hp, single overhead cam (SOHC) engine. The car also had MacPherson struts, and a stabilizer bar like the Super Beetle. Designers added a rear V-profile independent torsion beam axle with integral sway bar and trailing arms for a smooth, solid ride. *Road & Track* magazine claims that the New Beetle has a 0-60 mph (96 km/h) acceleration of 10.6 seconds.

Unlike the old Beetle, the New Beetle was not cheap. It retailed for $15,200 in 1998. Strong demand meant many dealers could charge more than that. Some reports had cars selling for up to $4,000 over the sticker price. There was also a Turbo Direct Injection (TDI) model available for a retail price of $16,475. A New Beetle convertible became available in 2003.

Volkswagen executives hoped the New Beetle would help the company reclaim a chunk of the American market. It did. New Beetle sales topped 55,000 in 1998. They exceeded

80,000 cars in both 1999 and 2000. Sales of Volkswagen's other models increased, too. As the New Beetle was flying high, Volkswagen said goodbye to the old Beetle. The Mexico factory built its final standard Porsche-designed Beetle in August 2003.

The New Beetle's story is more than just sales figures. It is a story of how people and cars relate. Like the old Beetle before it, the New Beetle is a celebrity. It continues to turn heads. With its friendly smile, the Beetle keeps reminding people how fun a car can be.

Timeline

1931

Ferdinand Porsche creates the first design for Project 12. It is the beginning of the Beetle.

1932

Porsche builds the first prototype for the *Volksauto*. The car has a 1.2-liter radial five-cylinder engine mounted behind the rear axle.

1933

Adolph Hitler and Porsche meet in Berlin. They discuss a car for ordinary people.

1937

German soldiers test-drive modified versions of Porsche's prototype around Germany.

1938

Hitler lays the cornerstone for the KdF-Stadt, Germany, plant where the *Volkswagen* will be produced.

1939

World War II begins and the KdF-Stadt plant is converted to building military vehicles.

1945

Allies win World War II and KdF-Stadt is renamed Wolfsburg. The Wolfsburg plant is taken over by British forces. Volkswagens are produced for British officers.

1948
Heinz Nordhoff assumes leadership of Wolfsburg plant, increasing efficiency and productivity.

1955
The one millionth Beetle is produced at the Wolfsburg plant. Volkswagen of America is established.

1968
U.S. Beetle sales peak at 569,292.

1969
Walt Disney comes out with the movie, *The Love Bug*.

1971
Super Beetle comes on the market.

1977
The standard Beetle stops being sold in the U.S.

1979
Beetle convertible sales in the U.S. end.

1994
Concept 1 (New Beetle) is shown at the North American International Auto Show.

1998
The New Beetle appears on the market.

2003
Standard Beetle production ends.

Glossary

Allied: the nations that fought against Germany in World War II.

chancellor: the leader of Germany.

cult: a group of like-minded people.

dictator: someone who has complete control of a country, often ruling it unjustly.

marks: German form of money before the Euro.

nonconformist: a person who does not go along with the usual trends.

prototype: the first version of an invention that tests an idea to see if it will work.

recess: to move back or down.

salvage: to rescue property from disaster.

World War II: 1939 to 1945, fought in Europe, Asia, and Africa. The United States, France, Great Britain, the Soviet Union, and their allies were on one side. Germany, Italy, Japan, and their allies were on the other side. The war began when Germany invaded Poland. The United States entered the war in 1941 after Japan bombed Pearl Harbor, Hawaii.

Internet Sites

www.abdopub.com

Would you like to learn more about the Beetle? Please visit
www.abdopub.com to find up-to-date Web site links about the
Beetle and other Ultimate Cars. These links are routinely monitored
and updated to provide the most current information available.

Index